BEDFORDSHIRE

Edited by Lucy Jeacock

First published in Great Britain in 2000 by
YOUNG WRITERS
Remus House,
Coltsfoot Drive,
Peterborough, PE2 9JX
Telephone (01733) 890066

HB ISBN 0 75432 220 3
SB ISBN 0 75432 221 1

FOREWORD

This year, the Young Writers' Up, Up & Away competition proudly presents a showcase of the best poetic talent from over 70,000 up-and-coming writers nationwide.

Successful in continuing our aim of promoting writing and creativity in children, our regional anthologies give a vivid insight into the thoughts, emotions and experiences of today's younger generation, displaying their inventive writing in its originality.

The thought, effort, imagination and hard work put into each poem impressed us all and again the task of editing proved challenging due to the quality of entries received, but was nevertheless enjoyable. We hope you are as pleased as we are with the final selection and that you continue to enjoy *Up, Up & Away Bedfordshire* for many years to come.

CONTENTS

Fahrat Nisa Shah	18
Anthony Hart	18
Kevin Francis	19
Callum Murnane	20
Farrah Gonsalves	20
Mariessa Joseph	21
Ahkeb Hussain	21
Thohaib Zia	22
Imran Ali Arif	22
Usman Uppal	23
Samantha Uren	23
Kainaat Qadri	24
Emma Catterson	24
Mystie Long	25
Anam Sajjad	25
Zain Ali	26
Maria Uddin	26
Taja Smith	27
Imran Salam	27
Hannah Rovner	28
Asad Ali Shah	28

Pirton Hill Junior School

Callum Riordan	29
Stephanie Ward	29
James Ward	30
Dannielle Fox	30
Daron Gunner	31
Ishtiyaa Shah	31
Danielle Sullivan	32
Robyn Thompson	32
Anne Folan	33
Gemma Hyde	33
Natasha Steele	34
Kimberley Coulson	34
Brendan Yates	35
Christopher Carpenter	35
Scarlet Lincoln	36

Mark McDade	56
Ross Mcsavaney	56
Paul Ayling	56
Michael Berni	57
Daniel McCarthy	57
Daniel Cubberley	58
Kim Oldham	58
Ashley O'Neill	59
Andrew Bywaters	59
Jayna Kirankumar Patel	60
Sharelle Bailey	60
Louisa Hunt	61
Antonio Brownie	61
Emma Corken	62
Lauren Berry	62
Sarah Connolly	63
Jason Callender	63
Christopher Gibson	64
Laura Ayres	64
Mumataz Islam	65
Matt Ingram	65
Lisa Tott	66
Nikki Hetherington	66
Alannah Gray	67
Oliver Thomson	67
Christopher Green	68

St Matthew's Junior School, Luton

Leah Waller	68
Erin Campbell	68
Saba Salim	69
Suki Eaton	69
Nathan Lomath	70
David Brooks	70
Jamie Maltman	70
Natasha Cooper	71
Charlotte Hardy	71
Nina Petrou	72

Rachel Pinckney	72
Shamaka Chandramohan	72
Jodie Innes	73
Thomas Hall	73
Martha Inch	74
Karly Lewis	74
Katharine Knight	75
Abigail Lamptey	76
Sara Dennehy	76
Beckie Holmes	77
Danielle King	77
Sally Cao	78
Holly Waterton	78

Sundon Park Junior School

Kate Blanckensee	79
Kenny Hill	79
Vicky Price	80
Jamie Birch	80
Steven Hicks	81
Richard Burton	81
Rebecca Matthews	82
Asaadar Rikaby	82
Sarah Potter	83
Zena-Marie Adams	83
Antony Graham	84
Mark Everritt	84
Samantha Robinson	85
Humayra Khan	85
Sarah Cutler	86
Zoe Jackson	86
Chloe King Lee	87
Kristian Currington	87
Charlene Mitchell	88
Christina Sibley	88
Krista Price	89
Chloe Chin	89
Gemma Donoghue	90

Weatherfield School

Sophie Collings	91
Gareth Glanville	91
Zoe Evangelou	91
Brandon Fudge	92
Helen Sanger	92
Daniel Wells	92
Luke Hignell	93
Andrew Golds	93

William Austin Junior School

Makedah Rose	94
Sebastian Paine	94
Nicola Ayres	95
Qays Akhtar	96
Sadaf Batool	96
Christine Mulvihill	97
Saresh Mehboob	97
Stacey Simmons	98
Chloé Fensome	98
Daniel Gregory	99
Nadine Awan	99
Farzanah Rana	100
Courtny Harper	100
Luke Middleton	101
Iram Hussain	101
Dale Driscoll	102
Jasprit Hayre	102
Sheri Bowers	103
Naweed Darr	104
Sadia Shabir	104
Jabbar Shah	105
Almas Ghafoor	106
Saira Miah	106
Sanya Akhtar	107
Zainab Muneer	108
Ricky Shah	108
Fabian Statchwell	109

The Poems

MILLENNIUM BUG?

The Millennium Bug goes all about
Gets drunk in the pub when he goes there.
One day this bug shrunk so small
He could not drink anymore.
This bug had had enough of this so
Went on to the computers.

The Millennium Bug went down the street
To find some computers to beat up.
He went in a room and saw them.
This bug crawled inside and hugged and
Killed the computer.
So that is why it is called the Millennium Bug.

Rachel Hyde (9)

CANDLE

At the beginning, when lit, it's bright,
Like a light.
It sways in the air like a polar bear!
It's blue, orange, yellow, red.
Just like a night light in bed.
It's calm and lovely the flame,
Like a man named Blain.
It twinkles in the light.
It will sway in the air tonight.
It's fluttering on wax,
The smell makes you relax.
A peaceful thing, delights you in the night.
It's calm, as bright as a light.

James-Anthony Burroughs (9)
Ferrars Junior School

SHERBET LEMON (ECHOING TASTE)

When I buy a sherbet lemon,
I unwrap the glowing wrapper and put it in my mouth.
I know the taste divine
Divine!
I suck all the sherbet out.

After school I buy some more,
To taste the flavour I adore.
The taste divine!
I eat my friend's and I eat mine.
I taste the flavour that I love,
Nice and sweet just like a dove.
The taste that no sweet could replace!
The flavour!
That echoing taste!
That forever stays in my mouth!
The eye-catching colour, the lovely taste,
The tangy scent of lemon, the echoing taste!
Oh that tangy echoing taste.

André Richards (9)
Ferrars Junior School

SHERBET LEMON

When I have a sherbet lemon and put it in my mouth,
I just lick and lick until all the sherbet comes out.
I don't care if it's sun or rain,
I just enjoy it!
And tomorrow I'll do it again.

Steven Redmond (9)
Ferrars Junior School

SHERBET LEMONS

When I go to the cupboard,
I see lots of sherbet lemons.
I pick one,
That crackly one.
I pick up the sweet,
Shut the cupboard.
I look at the wrapper,
Open the packet,
Feel the bumpy, juicy, sticky sweet.
Then I pop it in my mouth,
Suck, suck, suck!
Then I start to chew,
Chew, chew, chew!
Soon it's all gone.
I can't wait until tomorrow!

Amanda Smith (8)
Ferrars Junior School

SHERBET LEMON

The paper is crunchy and crackly and yellow and bumpy.
When I get home, I can't wait to eat some!
It is fizzy, like something frying in the pan.
The powder is like dust.
It has a lovely flavour.
It's juicy and sour but delicious to suck.

Benjahaman Browne (8)
Ferrars Junior School

CANDLE

It flickers in the moonlight.
It is very bright.
I can't help but notice,
The beautiful scent.

It is very romantic,
Shadowy and most beautiful.
So when I put it on the coffee table,
It silently creeps around the room.
I can feel the warmth
Tingling up my back.

It flickers silently around
The room.
It is very waxy and hot.
And very handy,
Because it helps us
Through a powercut.

Stacey Adams (9)
Ferrars Junior School

SHERBET LEMON

The sweet sat in my hand and it crackled
When I opened it. It was very sticky. So
I put it in my mouth and sucked it, until
It went very small and then I swallowed it!

Yeliz Tacel (8)
Ferrars Junior School

CANDLE

·O candle how you burn,
Your hot smell makes me doze,
When I think of you,
Slowly you melt away.

Misty and silent your love shows,
How I wonder how you glow.
Your shadow blends with others,
Flickering flame blow in the wind.

How you travel round the room,
How you don't make a sound.
All night long you flutter and blow,
Your scent flew away in the moonlight.

Jemma Oatley (8)
Ferrars Junior School

SHERBET LEMON

Sherbet lemon
Melts in me mouth.
All round me mouth
It's sweet.
It's hard, crunchy, melting
And sharp.
Sherbet lemon sure is neat.

Lewis Marshall (9)
Ferrars Junior School

CANDLELIGHT

When I look at a candle,
It flickers soft and bright,
And it reminds me
Of Christmas night.

I look into its glowing flame,
And watch it burning down,
It gives me memories of good times
And takes away my frown.

Its pointy shadow flickers,
And makes me have a sleepy yawn,
As I nod off into nightfall world
And wait for morning dawn.

Rebecca Miller (9)
Ferrars Junior School

SHERBET LEMONS

Thy only good thing about sherbet lemon.
It fizzes all around me mouth.
Sticky and juicy sherbet lemon.
Me mouth goes sour.
Me get yellow tongue.
Me love thy sherbet lemon.

Katrina Russell (8)
Ferrars Junior School

LIKE A CANDLE FLAME

Like a candle flame flickering,
Small in our darkness.
Uncreated light shines
Through junior eyes.
But they still they are still learning
Just because his light has shone.

Now we praise God,
That he will shine for our eyes,
Because they are eager to learn.
Just because of that light
From that candle flame.
So praise him, praise him
For that candlelight
That helps us learn.

Joshua Williams (8)
Ferrars Junior School

SHERBET LEMONS

It's golden yellow with sherbet in.
It makes me mouth water
Even when it's dry.
It makes me feel like
A hot sunny day.
It's fizzy and fruity
And melts away.

Kayleigh McDevitt (8)
Ferrars Junior School

SHERBET LEMON

I had a sherbet lemon
It sent me to sweetie heaven
It fizzled on me tongue
Right down to me tum
It made me eyes go pop
And sent me hippity-hop.

The citrus fruits
Have reached me boots
Now it tastes very fruity
It's sending me loopy
Now it has all gone
I'm heading off home.

Michael Janes (9)
Ferrars Junior School

CANDLES BURNING

When I light a candle it makes me calm.
Relaxed.
The melting wax trickles down the side of the soothing candle.
It's delightful.
When it changes shape, it sways in the air.
Delightful as can be and twinkling like a star.
The flame is brightening and eye-catching always.
Now it's fluttering with delight.

Thomas Smith (9)
Ferrars Junior School

CANDLE

Whenever I light a candle,
It starts to sway in the air.
It's okay.
Mmmm, I can smell that wonderful fragrance!
It twinkles like treacle!
When you are stressed,
Just light a candle!
Don't worry about the rest!
It sparkles in the dark at night.
Don't worry!
You won't get a fright!
The candle melts like a chocolate bar that has been in the warm sun.
Every candle makes us dream of a fantasy.

Leigh-Anne Matthews (8)
Ferrars Junior School

CANDLES!

I look at my candle,
It sparkles.
The wax is melting.
The flame is shining like the sun.
Now the wax has made a puddle.
It flutters like a bird's wing.
The colour is delightful.
Now, the candle is out.
I can't wait to light it up again.

Michael Blanchard (9)
Ferrars Junior School

WHAT ARE CLOUDS!

A huge comfortable fluffy bed,
in the sky moving around the world.

An enormous ball of wool all stuffed together,
but it's white, not pink and bigger.

Candyfloss being taken from a machine,
good and tasty as well.

A gigantic marshmallow swirling around,
large and small, there are different sizes.

A huge soft blanket that covers the sky,
it's fluffy and pleasant to feel.

David Bliss-Mcgrath (10)
Foxdell Junior School

MY LONELY WORLD

I sit and wait
I hesitate
What to do
It's getting late
I have no money
Just an empty plate
Time passes by
At such slow rate
My world is lonely
I need a mate
I am but a beggar
And this is my fate.

Amena Ahmed (11)
Foxdell Junior School

DRIVING

People drunk,
feet controlling,
men wobbling,
wheels rolling.

Car chasing,
children running,
car honking,
people humming.

Men staring,
tyres whooshing,
bicycles slipping,
drivers pushing.

Fasil Rehman (10)
Foxdell Junior School

THE WITCH'S SPELL

Frog's legs, bat's ears,
Cat's blood, snail's tear,
Chicken's wings, human's liver,
Enough to make you shiver!

Pig's bones, rat's nose,
Lizard's veins, bear's paws,
Dragon's teeth, hog's tail,
Worm's maw, fish's scales.

Bubble, bubble, mix about,
Stir it fast or I'll shout!

Nisha Parmar (10)
Foxdell Junior School

MY MAGIC BOX

I will put in the box
a lump of gleaming gold
a piece of paper as round as it can be

I will put in the box
a beautiful butterfly
a bottle of the finest wine in India

My box is
from out of space
a huge red ruby

I will put my box
in the deepest sea
in a safe, in the sea
in a safe in the wall.

Timothy Cakebread (9)
Foxdell Junior School

FOOD POEM

I like telly,
My dad hates jelly.
My brother does not eat custard,
My sister will never eat mustard.
I like cheese,
But my mum says eat peas.
I hate lemonade,
'Cause it's fizzy and has a lovely shade
And it goes pop!

Qamar Ahmed Khalid (8)
Foxdell Junior School

THE MAGIC BOX

I will put in my box . . .
The wicked eye watching of a witch,
The swish and swirling of a broom,
The giant growl of a lion.

I will put in my box . . .
The blowing and bellowing of an elephant,
The glittering silver star,
The loud laughing of a hyena.

My box is made out of . . .
The lovely skin of a leopard.
The key is made out of a dragon's nail.

I will put my box . . .
High up in the bright blue sky.

Shafaq Hoor Rathore (9)
Foxdell Junior School

THE MAGIC BOX

I will put in the box
bright colours of a rainbow
the beautiful song of birds
the stars shining light.
My box is made of shining gold
and stars on top.
Inside is darkness.
It looks like a magic box.
I will put my box underground in a hole in a wood.

Israr Khan (9)
Foxdell Junior School

THE BOGEY MAN'S LAIR

Deep, deep where you'll dare to go
the bogey man lurks in his dark, dark lair.

The place is forbidden! Some people
have been there but have never come back.

There are savage animals that eat you
if you're not plump enough for the bogey man.

Bones are roaming around everywhere
just waiting to give you a massive *scare!*

There are bugs crawling all over your face
from place to place.

Daniel Jeffries (8)
Foxdell Junior School

THE BOGEY MAN'S HOME

Deep, deep down in a forbidden place
The bogey man lurks waiting to show his face.

If you go down there you are in for a surprise
Because he just might open his eyes.

He lives in a place far away
Where no children go to play.

It is very dirty and dark
And it's near a children's park.

If you go in, it will give you a shiver
He might even eat your liver.

Eloise Wilkin (9)
Foxdell Junior School

ALL SORTS OF LESSONS

. A lesson of language,
Poems and stories of lands far, far away,
Visiting Stephenson's Treasure Island,
Or imagining travelling through the stars.

A lesson of numbers and shapes,
Shapes of every sort and kind,
Hexagons, triangles and squares,
Numbers from one to infinity,
Let's hope we get there.

A lesson of colours merging into pictures,
Paints and pastels of every hue,
Imaging the 'Mona Lisa',
Know that a picture paints a thousand words.

A lesson about the world we live in,
Countries spread far and wide,
America, India and Australia,
Taking in the incense upon the wind,
Standing under the 'Taj Mahal'.

A lesson of the past of mankind,
Ancient Rome, Athens and Cairo,
Pyramids at Giza and the Valley of the Dead,
The Roman and Greek Empires reigned,
Upon the world as they grew and grew.

As you walk through the classroom door,
Just imagine you're travelling through the stars,
Or you're on the ocean floor,
You're the one that makes learning fun.

Jaison Patel (11)
Foxdell Junior School

15

A Spell To Turn Someone Into A Frog

Bone of human, eye of dog
Lung of cats and swelt of frog.

Dragon's tail and shell of snail
Ear of goat and mouse's tail.

Fillet of snake
Then let it bake.

Scram, scram, ham and scribbles
Wait until the dormouse dribbles.

Now your spell is made
So don't let it fade.

Aqsa Ahmed (11)
Foxdell Junior School

Dinosaurs

Dinosaurs, dinosaurs, they're so cool,
Some are big and some are small,
They have big teeth which cut and chop,
They have big legs so it's hard to hop.
Some are green and some are brown,
They live in woods and not in town.
They roar and growl,
Their breath is foul.

Gareth Thomas (7)
Foxdell Junior School

THE CAT

Ferocious cat,
Creeping on her victim,
Dangerous cat,
Prowls on her victim,
With her sharp claws,
And her strong paws.

Playful cat,
Who chases her tail,
Gentle cat,
Who loves attention,
When you stroke her,
And tickle her.

Powerful cat,
Pounces on her victim,
Proud cat,
Stalking on her victim,
Playing on her victim,
About to attack her victim.

Contented cat,
Purring in front of the fire,
Cuddled cat,
Who washes herself with her pink tongue,
Who yawns to sleep,
And relaxes in front of the fire.

Taybah Fiaz (11)
Foxdell Junior School

THE MIGHTY SUN

The blazing sun in the sky,
Long, wavy, hair like flames,
Taking sunglasses off, look,
Of burning eyes.

Arms wide, legs stretched,
Hands open, shoulders back,
Spreading heat around people,
Giving energy to flowers, animals,
And plants.

She is powerful and mighty,
Not so cruel but scorching,
Wears a dress with matching,
Sun hat, puts sunglasses back on,
Which are made of shiny gold.

Her job is very important to us until the end of life.
She has a golden and beautiful face.

Fahrat Nisa Shah (11)
Foxdell Junior School

THE MAGIC BOX

I will put in the box
A flame-throwing Chinese dragon
A red claw-pinching crab
All the squidgy green peas in the world

I will put in the box
The icy weather of the winter months
Some sunbeams to keep me warm

My box is made out of wood
With metal gold at the corners
Of the wooden box and silver on
The faces of the box.

Anthony Hart (10)
Foxdell Junior School

THE TREE

It lives on land
It has lots of hands
It weights about a ton
It sometimes can be fun
It has things underground
It is easy to be found
It can live anywhere
It does not have any hair
It gives us lots of food
It also gives us wood
It always follows the sun
It does not need to run
It needs water to drink
It does not use the sink
It can be very tall
It also can be small
It is a home for birds
I cannot say words
Its flowers are nice to see
Its honey is for a bee
It gives us lots of shade
It is not man-made.

Kevin Francis (10)
Foxdell Junior School

THE MAGIC BOX

I will put in my box
A 13th month of the year
A tiger that is roaring for food
Stardust from space.

I will put in my box
All the gold in the world
A dragon made of steel
A witch that holds black magic.

My box is made of
Tiger's teeth, a bear's coat and steel.

I will put my box
In a safe and throw it in the sea.

Callum Murnane (9)
Foxdell Junior School

DAYS OF THE WEEK

Monday is a boring day, back to school again.
Tuesday is a new day, I thought it was Friday, I wish.
Wednesday is a computer day, I wish I had PE.
Thursday yes! It's nearly Friday.
Friday yes Friday at last, the weekend is going to be great fun.
Saturday's the best day of the week. I wish I went somewhere nice.
Sunday is a boring day.
Oh no! I have to do my homework again.

Farrah Gonsalves (9)
Foxdell Junior School

MY MAGIC BOX

I will put in the box
The whizzy dizzy dance of the calm blue sea.
The gold and bold sun.
The drum beat of the rain on the windowpane.

I will put in the box
My rattling battling keyrings.
The best times with friends and family.
And all my tales I've told to my friends.

My box is
On the outside it's made of the burning gas of the sun.
It has a key made out of shells.
And on the inside it's made of exquisite silk.

I will put my box
On an imaginary sand
Inside a garden
In my head.

Mariessa Joseph (10)
Foxdell Junior School

THE SUN

The sun is very dazzling, it hurts my eyes.
The sun is very sparkling, it sparkles in the sea.
The sun is very important, it gives us light.
The sun is very beautiful, it is very hot.
I saw the sun rising in the morning
And in the night I saw it setting.

Ahkeb Hussain (9)
Foxdell Junior School

MY MAGIC BOX

I will put in my box
All of my medals that I earned for karate.
All of my money I got from France.
All of my secrets that I have in my diary.

I will put in my box
The biggest, goldest key in the world.
I will put my best friend, Sajid because he makes me happy
And always there for me.
I will put my diary that tells me the events that went on during the year.

My box
Is made out of the hardest silvery steel.
Is made out of a spaceship with a pointy edge.
Is made out of a chain, hard and gold.

I will put my box
In a treasure chest and throw it in the sea.
Underground and dig it hard down.
In the middle of the earth.

Thohaib Zia (10)
Foxdell Junior School

LION

There was a lion named Fred,
He had big razor teeth,
But he had small razor sharp claws,
Everyone called him a wimp,
As he was afraid of everything,
Except for human beings.

Imran Ali Arif (11)
Foxdell Junior School

THE TRAIN JOURNEY

Clickety click clickety click
Under a bridge beside a hedge
Zooming past sights, with a wink of an eye.

Clackety clank clackety clank
Flashing by whizzing by
Faster than the Concords fly
Swaying left swaying right
In the depths of a dark dark night.

. Clickety click clackety clank
Stop at a station
Reached our destination
Sssssshhhhhh!

Usman Uppal (11)
Foxdell Junior School

TASTY FOOD

I like lovely long spaghetti
slimy, juicy and very slippery.

I like lovely lemonade
it fizzes on your tongue
and makes you burp.

I like pizza
it's hot and yummy.

But I hate onion!
It's sour and spicy.

Samantha Uren (7)
Foxdell Junior School

IT'S THE SUN

It's got flaming hair,
Burning eyes,
Hopping feet and never lies,
He's hot, wet and sticky,
Just like tar,
He's the biggest star.

He's round and wiggles,
And always giggles,
Sparkles and sprinkles,
Burns and shines,
Walks and talks,
Wobbles and gobbles,
Stinks and sweats,
It's the sun,
Having fun.

Kainaat Qadri (10)
Foxdell Junior School

YEAR 2000

When it was the countdown 10, 9, 8
We all got in a circle by the gate.
We started to shout
10, 9, 8, 7, 6, 5, 4, 3, 2, 1, 0
Bang! Bang!
Went the fireworks outside the door.
You want to see the state of the floor!

Emma Catterson (8)
Foxdell Junior School

WHEN I GROW UP I WANT TO BE A VET

When I grow up I want to be a vet.
Mummy won't let me have a pet.
My Auntie Susanna bought me a mouse.
Mum said no Mystie! I'm not having that in my house.
When I grow up I want to be a vet.
I mean when I'm older, I'm not clever enough yet.
The main thing is, I love all animals, big and small.
One's that slither, hop, fly, swim and crawl.
Dogs and cats, wolves and cheetahs.
Tame or wild, I'll look after all God's creatures.
I don't want to be a hairdresser, a secretary or an air hostess.
When I grow up I'm going to be the best ever vet.

Mystie Long (8)
Foxdell Junior School

IF YOU . . .

If you had an accident, what are you going to claim?
If you had an accident, who are you going to blame?

If you were going to play, what are you going to say?
If you were going to play, are you going to give your horse a little bit of
hay?

If you were going to a party, what are you going to wear?
If you were going to a party, what are you going to hear there?

If you were going to sleep, where are you going to peep?
If you were going to sleep, where are you going to creep?

Anam Sajjad (9)
Foxdell Junior School

THE BOOGIE MAN!

Don't scream,
Don't shout,
And don't touch the music . . .

Music is fun but you better run,
Behind the nice tune,
Is a nasty truth,
He takes your heart through the sound,
The beat takes over,
When you let the music play,
Listen too long and you're sure to be gone,
He will wrap you in his sweet melody,
Then in his trance you are . . .
Before you know it you're in his power to devour.

Yes, he is of course . . .
        The Boogie man!

Zain Ali (11)
Foxdell Junior School

FLOWER

I saw a flower in the park,
It was nearly dark,
The wind was blowing,
While the flower was growing,
It was yellow and brown,
I was sitting on the ground.

Maria Uddin (10)
Foxdell Junior School

MY MAGIC BOX

I will put in the box
A shiny clear crystal.
A sweet delicious candy land.
A hard metal treasure chest.

I will put in the box
My white wobbly teeth.
A sunny enjoyable holiday.
A soft furry canary bird.

My box is
A brown chocolate box.
A shiny gleaming cloth.
A box made of pure gold.

I will put my box
Under my bed. ·
A secret place in the attic.
Under the ground.

Taja Smith (10)
Foxdell Junior School

SPRING POEM

B,dong, b,dong, my spring keeps on bouncing,
leaping and jumping high into the sky.
The spiralling and twisting beautifully,
spring high and fast.
B,dong, b,dong flowing gracefully in its never-ending shape,
it goes in patiently curling.

Imran Salam (10)
Foxdell Junior School

MY BEST FRIEND

My best friend's name is Billy,
In the rain he gets very chilly.

He likes dinosaurs bigger,
I like Winnie the Pooh's friend, Tigger.

He has a dog named Sunny,
Billy is very funny!

He is naughty,
He is a shorty!

He hates school, not like I,
For his tea he has pie!

He likes chocolate, so do I,
So say bye-bye!

Hannah Rovner (9)
Foxdell Junior School

WALKING

Walking through the breeze that gave us a freeze,
Walking through the grass that was made out of brass,
Walking through the fields protected by shields,
Walking through the mud that was piles of floods,
Walking through the sea, that was covered with fleas,
Walking through the stones, I saw plenty of bones,
Walking through the gate, had no mates,
Walking through the beads, had no seeds,
Walking through the wet, had no bet,
Walking through the books, had no looks.

Asad Ali Shah (10)
Foxdell Junior School

HANDS

Magicians have magically marvellous,
magnificent hands.
Agents have action-packed, aiming,
adult hands.
Builders have unbreakable, bulky,
busy hands.
Clowns have clumsy, curious,
comical hands.

Wow! Their hands are busy . . .
very busy.

Callum Riordan (8)
Pirton Hill Junior School

PLEASE GEMMA

I will remember you wherever you are.
Please Gemma come back soon.
Your eyes twinkle like the moon.
Please Gemma come back soon.
Remember we used to play every single day.
Please Gemma come back soon.
I will love you no matter what.

Please Gemma
come
back soon.

Stephanie Ward (9)
Pirton Hill Junior School

ANIMALS SAFARI

Animals nice
Animals ugly
Animals huge
Animals tiny
Animals friendly
Animals house
Animals tail
Animals fast
Animals slow
Animals cunning
Animals beauty
Animals tall
Animals hall
Animals noisy
Animals hide
And the best thing of all is the bath at the end of the day.

James Ward (9)
Pirton Hill Junior School

LOST

Where's Mum?!
I'm stuck in town
Alone and terrified
Don't know what to do, where to go
She's gone!

Dannielle Fox (8)
Pirton Hill Junior School

I AM THERE

I see the red on a heart,
I see your red fluffy coat,
I see the rainbow in the sky,
I think of the glitter in your eye.

I am there, don't think I'm dead,
I am the shelter over your head,
My spirit is near,
Don't forget, I am here.

Don't cry and weep,
I am in peace,
I'm always there,
I love and I care.

Do not forget
I am there.

Daron Gunner (10)
Pirton Hill Junior School

LOST

Shopping
With Mum and Dad
A busy town centre
Turn around, suddenly they're gone!
Oh no!

Ishtiyaa Shah (8)
Pirton Hill Junior School

FUNKY FEET

At school my feet do
Wobbly walking,
Hippy hopping,
Running rapidly,
Scary skipping.
My feet can do
Clicking crackling,
Kicking quickly.
My feet look like
Funky fries,
Fantasy feet.
My socks are
Smelly socks,
Stinky socks.

Danielle Sullivan (8)
Pirton Hill Junior School

I MISS YOU GRANNY

I miss you, Granny, every day,
My heart wonders if you are okay.
You write me letters
And ring on the phone
And give me toys
That I can cuddle at home.
I miss you, granny, wherever I am,
Even at school or in the playground.

Robyn Thompson (9)
Pirton Hill Junior School

THE STARS

The stars come out at night,
and are very bright.
They are very high,
way up in the sky.
Shining out their light,
they twinkle with all their might.
Catch them you can try,
but you will only cry.
They are very white,
Mars is to the right.
Oh my!
You sigh.

Anne Folan (10)
Pirton Hill Junior School

RAINBOW COLOURS

Rainbow colours are so beautiful
They light up the sky and make it look wonderful.
So if you see a rainbow think of the colours
And you might win it.
The rainbow has a very nice shade of yellow and blue
So look at a rainbow and see the beautiful colours.
A rainbow will make you feel so wonderful.

The rainbow colours are beautiful.

Gemma Hyde (11)
Pirton Hill Junior School

CINDERELLA

Cinderella get my clothes clean,
I have to wash,
Cinderella get my make-up,
Here I have to fetch their make-up,
Cinderella get my food,
I have to feed them,
Cinderella get my jewellery now,
I have to even dress them,
Cinderella serve me,
I even have to serve them,
Cinderella
What now?
Clean the toilets,
I'm getting out of here,
Goodbye!

Natasha Steele (10)
Pirton Hill Junior School

HEADTEACHERS ARE REAL

Playgrounds only hide the true terror inside.
Books - are tatty, books are long, books are a teacher's only friend.
Dinners - are worse, dinners are gruel, dinners are always in the hall.
Teachers - have pets, which are always the best.
Blackboards - are old, blackboards are bold, they hold secrets to classes
of gold.
Headteachers - are real! Headteachers seal! The horrors of *school!*
Oh cool.

Kimberley Coulson (11)
Pirton Hill Junior School

COOL FRIEND

My friend is cool,
when he plays games and loses,
he cries
and refuses to wipe his eyes.
There's one thing I hate,
when he says that
he's the best.
He takes off his shirt, I can see his vest.
Well that's not all,
once he fell from a wall,
I began to laugh.
He got up and called me a giraffe.
He always pretends to be a monkey swinging
from tree to tree.
He says it's an impression of me.

Brendan Yates (11)
Pirton Hill Junior School

MY COMPUTER

Frustrating when you can't do it,
but wonderful when you can,
if there's more than one way,
you'll come up with a plan.

When there's corny catchphrases,
they always make you laugh,
falling off your chair,
it's time for a bath.

I'm talking about my computer!

Christopher Carpenter (11)
Pirton Hill Junior School

WILL YOU REMEMBER ME?

Will you remember me?
Remember me
Will you remember me?
Forever
When the roses sprout
And the sea splashes
Against the rocks
Do not cry
I can see it in your eyes
Please, please
Remember me
Would I see
The sound of the sea?
Remember me.

Scarlet Lincoln (10)
Pirton Hill Junior School

I STILL REMEMBER YOU, GRAN

I still remember you, Gran
With your old frying pan
The way you cooked eggs, sausages
Bacon and chips
The way you make the pancake flip
I remember your hair when I see a fuzzy bear
Don't forget, Gran I still remember you

Luke Pacquette (9)
Pirton Hill Junior School

MY IMAGINARY FRIEND

My imaginary
friend has a big
green hat and
a short and
stumpy, fat head
with a big round
chin.
He has two big
arms which can reach his toes and he looks
like a penguin.
His body is
like a tree
stump, it's short
and broad,
and has a voice
like the scream
of a girl!

Dhaval Panchal (10)
Pirton Hill Junior School

GREAT NAN

I sit under the sparkling sky.
The stars remind me of you, great Nan.
The clock that sat on the mantelpiece.
The summer's sun in the flat.
Sitting in your rocking chair by
The window in the world.

Steven Rowley (9)
Pirton Hill Junior School

CINDERELLON

Cinderellon, Cinderellon,
Do the castle,
Do the castle,
Tidy it up!
Tidy it up!
Cinderellon, Cinderellon,
Do my bedroom,
Do my bedroom,
Tidy it now!
Tidy it now!
Cinderellon, Cinderellon,
Wash Lucifer,
Wash Lucifer,
Now!
Now!
Cinderellon, Cinderellon

Barry Snelling (10)
Pirton Hill Junior School

THE WAR

Guns being shot, high and low,
Men are running, nowhere to go,
People shouting, be calm, be calm,
Some men were lucky but with only one arm,
Men being shot, fall down on the floor,
People falling more and more,
We now wear poppies for the things they've done.
We will always remember each and every one.

Chloe Pettengell (11)
Pirton Hill Junior School

MY BEST FRIEND

Me and my friend like swimming.
Playing bat and ball.
We also like sunbathing.
Sometimes she drives me up the wall.
When she eats ice-cream,
She gets it round her mouth.
When we walk out on the street,
We always head south.
Sometimes
We play Barbie at
Five o'clock at night.
Sometimes
We have a tournament.
I always win the fight.
She beats me at tennis.
I'm worse than a tree.
But all I know is that she's friends with me.

Louise Randall (11)
Pirton Hill Junior School

REMEMBER GRANDAD

I remember you when I go to your grave.
You were tall and skinny and you smoked a lot.
Why did you start smoking?
I remember when you came to my house every Wednesday.
You gave me sweets every time.
I remember when you had cancer
Because of smoking and died.
We can't do those things anymore.

Keval Shah (10)
Pirton Hill Junior School

THE SCARY HOUSE

Step in through the enormous spiky gates -
Be quiet as a mouse.
We're going to sneak, and take a peek,
Inside the scary house!

Ghosts are howling in the hallway.
Ghastly creatures spitting on the stairs.
Imps and spirits have frightening fights.
I wait to catch them in their flares!

In the kitchen there's a scary wizard,
Making a potion with spider pies.
They're for a very special meal -
A Valentine's surprise!

A metal empty suit of shining armour,
Is clanking loudly down the stairs,
To a disco in the other room -
It's the monsters all in pairs.

So while the disco is in full dance,
Be quiet as a mouse.
Tiptoe out when it's loud -
Escape from the scary house!

Tanisha Darji (8)
Pirton Hill Junior School

SPORT

Golf if good!
Basketball's better,
I like football!
Whatever!

Rugby balls are egg-shaped,
Footballs are round,
Golf balls are tiny,
They can't be found!

Paul Stiff (9)
Pirton Hill Junior School

MY TEACHER

My teachers shares
Respect,
That I like a lot,
She listens to my problems with
Ears.

My teacher is a lovely
Person if
She's not in a mood
(Red-faced
Short-tempered,
Nasty,
And rude!)

Her hair is a wacky way,
With her groovy clips,
And big wicked high
Boots.

Of course it has got to
Be my teacher.

Donna Craig (11)
Pirton Hill Junior School

POEMS

P oems make you laugh
O r they make you cry,
E very time I read one,
M y mum says to me to watch the clouds go by,
S ometimes I really think I will die.

Dean Sutton (10)
Pirton Hill Junior School

BEST FRIENDS

We like to play sport and he is good at it.
We sleep at each other's house.
He likes to eat vindaloo.
He is good and bad.
We like to call each other names.
But we always make up.
He can be stupid sometimes.

John Lawrence (11)
Pirton Hill Junior School

SHARK!

A shark is a barbaric huge fish
It can smell food on a dish
When you see one you should *dart!*
It can snap, it can bite
Beware you're in for a scare.

James Dalgarno (10)
Pirton Hill Junior School

FOUL FEET

My feet are making my
Shoes shake,
Socks smell,
Toes timid.

On the street my feet
Stamp sulkily,
Stop stubbornly,
Feet flee.

. At home my feet are always
Running restlessly,
Jumping joyfully.

Bryony Coombs (8)
Pirton Hill Junior School

FOOD

Big, bouncy bananas in the bowl
Chocolate chip ice-cream
Pizza is huge in boxes
Perfect cool pie warming up
Ice-cream is cold
Juicy apple in my mother's tum
Green huge peas cooking in a pan
Chunky cheese in sandwiches
Ham and salad cream on toast.

Kirsty Ralph (8)
Pirton Hill Junior School

THE CRAZY SHOPPING LIST

Trust my mum to think of her tum!
A silly shopping list
Oh no!

Cornish carrots,
Boldy bananas,
Silly sausages.

But that's just the beginning!

Purple peas,
Pink potatoes.

('I don't like pink,' I said, but did she listen?)

Burny bread,
Special sprouts (Yuck!)

I can't believe my mum, it hurts my tum!

Renate O'Connor (9)
Pirton Hill Junior School

MY FRIEND

There is a boy called Richard
Who is my best friend
I know he will be with me until the end
He's football mad and hockey sad
My best friend Richard

Liam Quince (11)
Pirton Hill Junior School

THE ANIMAL BOAT

Racing Rabbits,
Fast Frogs,
Hopping Hyenas,
When will they stop?
There's a Hare on the stair,
Aaah get it off.
Bear Blowing Bubbles,
When will this stop?
Kangaroos kicking everyone down.
A Fuzzy Fox,
A Grumpy Goat,
What is this house called?
The Animal Boat.

Keri Murphy (9)
Pirton Hill Junior School

THE ZOO

When I go to the zoo it's great but I don't really hate
The great big dozy giraffe,
Neither the hyena, trying to laugh.

When I go to the fierce ferocious farm I am trying to calm
The cheeky chubby chicks,
I'm even trying to calm the pigs!

When I go home to my own safari zone I see
Dozens of animals,
It's like I'm in Rome.

Kyle Earnshaw (8)
Pirton Hill Junior School

CINDERELLA

Cinderella, Cinderella,
Talks to mice,
Talks to mice,
Cinderella, Cinderella,
Is very nice,
Is very nice,
Cinderella, Cinderella,
Is very brave,
Is very brave,
Cinderella, Cinderella,
Has to work,
Has to work,
Cinderella, Cinderella,
Is a slave,
Is a slave,
Cinderella, Cinderella,
Has a cat,
Has a cat,
Cinderella, Cinderella,
Works just like that!
Works just like that!
Cinderella, Cinderella,
Has a dog,
Has a dog,
Cinderella, Cinderella,
Does not have a frog,
Does not have a frog,
Cinderella, Cinderella,
Helps the mice,
Helps the mice,

Cinderella, Cinderella,
Cries by night,
Cries by night,
Cinderella, Cinderella,
Will take flight,
Will take flight.

Claire Rushby (10)
Pirton Hill Junior School

PRICKLES

Prickles is a hedgehog,
Prickles loves to play.
Prickles loves to skip around,
And he skips all day.

Prickles is a hedgehog,
Prickles loves to play.
And he will skip around,
In the summer anyway.

Prickles is a hedgehog,
Prickles loves to play.
And he would skip for miles, and miles,
On the English Bay.

Prickles is a hedgehog,
Prickles loves to play.
Until it's time to hibernate,
Then on the leaves he lay.

Danielle O'Sullivan (11)
Pirton Hill Junior School

IN OUR CRAZY CLASSROOM

In our crazy classroom,
lots of crazy things are going on.
Like children flying like birds
and jumping like rabbits.
When will it stop?
In our crazy classroom,
lots of crazy things are going on.
Like children prancing like
Lions, tigers and leopards.
When will it stop?
Sometimes I think I'm in a zoo!
You never know . . .
someone might say
Moo!

Stephanie Russell (9)
Pirton Hill Junior School

REMEMBERING YOU

I cry and weep just for you,
When the winter trees are blowing,
I still remember you,
I see your picture looking at me,
And the smile too,
Your eyes are a twinkling light,
Which guides me through my darkest moments,
I remember you.

Pareena Shah (9)
Pirton Hill Junior School

ONE DAY AT SCHOOL

One day at school I lost my book
I asked everyone, even the cook.
One day at school I felt really ill,
I went really dizzy and felt sick on the hill.
One day at school we were making our pots,
We were meant to do stripes
But by accident I did dots.
One day at school in my lunch
There was a big spider
With a green tongue.
It was going to lick me
So I went in the glider.
One day after school
My mum's car broke down
So I had to walk home
With a big frown.

Roshni Sagoo (9)
Pirton Hill Junior School

GRANDAD

Grandad, Grandad I remember you, I do
I wish I could see you, I do, I do
Every moment I spent with you
I enjoyed being there with you

Now I'm here all alone
I cry, I cry all alone
Help me please
If you do

Stacey Lever (10)
Pirton Hill Junior School

DANGEROUS DINOSAURS

Dinosaurs are everywhere, under your bed,
in your dreams,
Dinosaurs are fast especially veloceraptors.
Later on they transport out of your head into
town ready to kill.
They destroy everything, cars, buildings, everything they touch.
It's up to me to destroy them, I
run up and fight but the T-rex
bashes me out the way but I remember it's a dream.
I wake up and ask my mum
'Has there been any dinosaurs?'
'Who would ask a silly question like that?'

James Lockyer (9)
Pirton Hill Junior School

I REMEMBER YOU

I remember you
When I see a black bear
I remember you
When I see a red, red rose
I remember you
When I walk past your old house
I remember you
When I take a trip to London
I remember you
When we do PE at school
I remember you
My best friend forever.

Loretta Seaton (9)
Pirton Hill Junior School

BROTHER

Even though I never saw you
I wish to see you once
I ask you just one question
Why did you go away?
why didn't you live a life
A life with me and your family
Even if you come back now
And be born as a newborn child
I will be really happy
And not so sad as I was
I imagine you playing with me
And our family happy as can be
Even through you're not down here
You still are with me and also in my heart!

Sneha Shah (9)
Pirton Hill Junior School

REMEMBER ME

Remember me
Like the sea
As calm as the waves
And not like the darkness of the caves
The tree you see outside your window
Is as free as me
I did not go low
Into the ground
And just remember I am around
So remember me

Cameron Devall (9)
Pirton Hill Junior School

MY BEST FRIEND

My friend plays football with me,
Once he went down and could not see,
He fell from a tree,
And broke his knee,
He can run,
As fast as a shot from a gun.

He eats an apple,
Before going to the chapel,
He prays all day,
And his favourite month is May.

We shout and scream,
When we run through the stream,
I don't know with I'll do,
Without my best friend Jordan.

Ricky McKeown (10)
Pirton Hill Junior School

FAMILIES

Mum - nice, cuddly, good for advice and always there for you.
Dad - good for football, good for advice (normally on football).
Sister - cute, sweet, always acts innocent and good
When you need to be told 'I love you'!
Nan - knitting Nan is what she's called,
Good when you're broke or need a present.
Grandad - computer cool is what he should be,
For he is a normal referee!

Liane Evenden (11)
Pirton Hill Junior School

PUPPIES FEVER

Puppies, puppies they're *so* fun,
Lovely,
Cute,
Extreme,
for everyone.

Puppies, puppies they're *so* warm,
Beautiful,
Kind,
Fluffy,
for everyone.

Puppies, puppies their love,
is like your *bestest*
Friend for *always*
a *lovely one!*

Lisa Forsyth (8)
Pirton Hill Junior School

I WILL REMEMBER YOU

I never really knew you
But I knew who you were
Wherever I go
I always know you'll be around
You're always in my thoughts
I will
Remember
You
Grandad

Stacey Deamer (9)
Pirton Hill Junior School

TEACHERS

Teachers are crazy.
Teachers are mad.
Teachers help children who are very bad.
Teachers work hard throughout the year.
Some teachers shout and some teachers cheer.
I think teachers are the best.
As teachers have taught me to do my best.

Shanade Collins (9)
Pirton Hill Junior School

MY DAD'S SOCKS

My dad's socks are smelly
My dad's socks stink like cheese
My dad's socks have steam coming out of them.
And he distracts me from my dangerous dream.
Oooo my dad's socks smell!

Keith Carroll (9)
Pirton Hill Junior School

SOMEONE

Someone I know is very tall,
On the 18th April he was born,
Many people love him,
Everybody remembers him,
Out of 100,000 he is the best,
Nobody hates him,
Everyone likes my grandad!

Lisa Coulson (11)
Pirton Hill Junior School

MY FRIEND

My friend is kind
because she lets me in her nan's house.
My friend is nice
because she can keep a secret.
My friend is thoughtful
because she lets me go to the pub with her.
My friend is nice
because she lets me have some of her sweets.
My friend can be nice to play with.
My friend is *Chantelle*.

Jadene Anderson (11)
Pirton Hill Junior School

LET ME REMEMBER YOU, MUM

Let me remember you, Mum
As I did before
You are like a jelly bean
Coming through the door.
Your snow white shoes
Caught my eye
Like a new born butterfly
For you are the prettiest girl
That I have known.

Eire May Dalgarno (10)
Pirton Hill Junior School

MY FRIEND

My friend he makes me laugh
And we play football.
I was on the floor
He picked up and scores.
At half time he was drinking wine.
Back on he was singing songs.
My friend he makes me laugh.

Mark McDade (11)
Pirton Hill Junior School

THE S POEM

On the sea I had a small shiny ship
which is sunk to the bottom of the ship sunk sea,
in the ship sunk sea there was as ship sunk sea shark
which loved to snap up some sea shore sailors
when she shore sharks gobbled up all the sea shore sailors
the sea shore sailors were never to be seen again.

Ross Mcsavaney (10)
Pirton Hill Junior School

MY FRIEND

My friend is fun.
My friend has a funny way of talking.
My friend makes me laugh.
My friend is special.
Can you guess him?
It is Brendan!

Paul Ayling (11)
Pirton Hill Junior School

CINDERELLA

Cinderella is bossed around,
In her home, in her home,
Not appreciated, not appreciated!
Don't fret, please don't fret,
Endless cleaning to be done, to be done,
Repeated cleaning, repeated cleaning,
Endless cleaning - all night long,
Lots to do!
Lots to do!
And at last finished! Zzzzzz.

Michael Berni (9)
Pirton Hill Junior School

DANIEL

D aniel is sooo happy
A nd so gentle,
N ever unhappy,
I n his mind he thinks football,
E xcellent is his middle name,
L ollys are his favourite sweets.

And how did I know that?
Because it's me!

Daniel McCarthy (11)
Pirton Hill Junior School

THE JICKLE JACKLE

I think I saw on the floor
A jickle jackle and heard it roar
Then I shut the door
Then it knocked on the door
And there he was, still on the floor
When he was there
He gave me such a scare
Growled like a bear
Saw bits of its own hair
Next I said go away
By the end of the day
The jickle jackle waved and went away.

Daniel Cubberley (9)
Pirton Hill Junior School

I REMEMBER YOU, GRANDAD

I remember you smiling and laughing
I remember the twinkle in your eyes
I remember you holding me in your arms
I remember I remember
I remember crying at your grave
I remember sitting under the trees with you
I remember you I remember you
I remember looking at the stars with you
I remember I remember
There you are up in heaven

Kim Oldham (10)
Pirton Hill Junior School

ONE BIG LEAP TO JUPITER

One day
I looked up in
the sky, I saw the stars
and the moon, I could not touch
them so I jumped and went into space. I
could see earth. I went to Jupiter and I went through
the atmosphere going down and down, it seemed like a
day till I hit the ground. I thought I was dead.
I was not, I went around the place,
I did not like it, I tried to get
away from the planet, I
jumped and jumped but
I came back down
again. I could
not get off.
I was stuck
on Jupiter.

Ashley O'Neill (11)
Pirton Hill Junior School

LIZZY'S BAD DAY

Lizzy was quite fizzy,
but she was very busy.
One day she lost her tracksuit,
and she only had one boot.
She couldn't do her daily jog
and to top it all she got bitten by a dog.

Andrew Bywaters (10)
Pirton Hill Junior School

MY DOG SAMMIE

My dog Sammie is
cute,
clever,
active and
fluffy.

My dog Sammie can
help you,
protect you,
love you and
play with you.

My dog Sammie can also be
a good pet,
noisy,
give you a lot of exercise and
be very messy and dirty too.

But my dog is the best dog in the whole
world.

Jayna Kirankumar Patel (8)
Pirton Hill Junior School

CINDERELLA

Cinderella, Cinderella what are you gonna do?
Cinderella, Cinderella they are spying on you.
Cinderella, Cinderella who wants to go to the ball.
Cinderella, Cinderella has now got grounded.
Cinderella, Cinderella.

Sharelle Bailey (10)
Pirton Hill Junior School

KOALA POEM

When you are a koala like me,
It's impossible not to make friends with you.
We climb about and sometimes swing,
And that's all we really do.

We are friendly and kind, you are not.
You cut down our trees.
It's hard to believe,
When you've got leaves up to your knees.

As if that's not enough,
You come to collect us.
To put us in zoos,
As if you really must.

Saba Salim (11)
St Matthew's Junior School, Luton

CRUNCHIE

Crunchies are brown,
bubbly, yummy,
scrumptious, crumbly,
honeycomb,
but the best thing about Crunchies
is that they melt in your mouth!
Some people don't like Crunchies,
I'll eat one any day.
So come to me today
for a Crunchie! Crunchie!

Suki Eaton (7)
St Matthew's Junior School, Luton

SNAKE!

Slither, slither, slither
Goes the slimy, slimy snake
Hissss goes the snake
Hisssing and hissssing and missing his prey
Trying to eat you up!

Nathan Lomath (8)
St Matthew's Junior School, Luton

SNAKE

The snake slithers.
The snake's tongue flickers in and out.
It once went round and ate its tail
And was never seen again

David Brooks (8)
St Matthew's Junior School, Luton

A KILLER WHALE

A killer whale
Is a big bad whale,
Long, black and white whale.
Some are friendly whales
And have sharp teeth!

Jamie Maltman (7)
St Matthew's Junior School, Luton

APPLES

There's an apple tree
In my garden
Bigger than me!
Bigger than my mum and
Bigger than my dad!
In autumn
It's full with green, fine apples.
I haven't tasted them
But they look so delicious!
Crunchy,   .
Juicy,
Round,
Smooth and
Hard.
I fell just like taking one now.
I love apples!

Natasha Cooper (7)
St Matthew's Junior School, Luton

WINTER

In winter all the snowflakes fall,
They all end up on top of the wall,
When winter is finally here,
I jump up with joy and fear,   ·
I'm so happy,
And would even like to wear a nappy!

Charlotte Hardy (8)
St Matthew's Junior School, Luton

SMELL

Oh! No! There's a smelly smell behind me!
Oh! No! There's footsteps behind me, tip tap, tip tap!
Oh! No! The footsteps are getting louder and louder
And the smell is getting nearer and nearer!

Nina Petrou (7)
St Matthew's Junior School, Luton

FURRY RABBIT

White, furry,
brown, fluffy,
smooth, soft.

Rachel Pinckney (7)
St Matthew's Junior School, Luton

WINTER

Winter is cold
Christmas trees are sold
To those who are bold
To go out in the cold.

Shamaka Chandramohan (8)
St Matthew's Junior School, Luton

WEATHER

Again it started to rain ·
Oh what a pain
I wish the sun was shining
But it was thundering and lightning

Again it started snowing
The sky was white
And the sky was as dark as night

Again it started hailing
My plans for the day were failing
I was going outside
But the sun decided to hide

Again it started to rain
What a pain
Enough water for a fish
Oh I wish I wish I wish.

Jodie Innes (8)
St Matthew's Junior School, Luton

BILL GATES (CLERIHEW)

Sir Bill Gates
Loves brown and soft dates,
He loves his money,
But it's turning him rather funny.

Thomas Hall (10)
St Matthew's Junior School, Luton

SEASONS

Spring is when the animals grow,
and the rivers begin to flow.
You will always know when it is spring,
because the birds start to sing.
Summer is so much fun,
because there is lots of sun.
The teachers don't have to teach,
because they're sitting on the beach.
When the autumn leaves fall,
they blow against the garden wall.
Winter is when some animals go to sleep,
and the sheep start to weep.
The cold wind makes your face glow,
especially when it starts to snow.

Martha Inch (8)
St Matthew's Junior School, Luton

SPAGHETTI

You suck me into your mouth with a slurp
I slither in the bowl
Round and round I go
I have a sauce which is orange
I'm like a snake but I don't eat animals
You eat me
What am I?
Spaghetti.

Karly Lewis (10)
St Matthew's Junior School, Luton

SEASONS

Spring.
Spring is freshness,
snow is lessness,
the flowers are growing,
the sun is glowing,
and the birds are restless.

Summer
Summer is playtime,
farmers haytime,
the flowers are blooming,
the bees are zooming,
all the long daytime.

Autumn
Autumn is golden,
its colour bolden,
leaves are swirling,
colourful, twirling,
jump up and hold them.

Winter
Winter is shivery,
cold air withery,
the leaves are no more,
the animals snore,
it's icy and slithery.

Katharine Knight (7)
St Matthew's Junior School, Luton

ORANG-UTANS

We are orang-utans,
We live in the jungle,
We swing in the trees,
Eating luscious leaves.

At night time,
We sleep in a line,
In comfy beds,
Right on the edge.

When we wake up,
We fall with a bang,
Not a very nice bump,
But we get up on our hands.

Abigail Lamptey (11)
St Matthew's Junior School, Luton

NONSENSE POEM

I saw a flock of fish flying
in the sky, one fell down and
hit me in the middle of my eye.

I saw a school of birds swimming in
the sea, one flipped up and bit me
in the middle of my knee.

I saw a slither of penguins
waddling in the sand, one ran
up and pecked me painfully on my hand.

Sara Dennehy (11)
St Matthew's Junior School, Luton

THE SPIDER

When you're a spider like me,
It's impossible to make friends with humans like you.
We're friendly and we don't cause any trouble,
You humans certainly do.

We crawl around on your floor,
Minding our own business
While you chase us around
With the Daily Telegraph.

If that doesn't succeed you try the slipper,
You smack it across the floor.
I lost my three brothers because of you,
They're all squashed on the floor.

Beckie Holmes (10)
St Matthew's Junior School, Luton

I SAW

I saw a rat eating chocolate
I saw a boy chewing a bone
I saw a dog laughing his head off
I saw a clown flying in the sky
I saw a bird sprinting along
I saw a cat playing the guitar
I saw Jimi Hendrix eating a chair
I saw a lion walking the high wire
I saw a man eating ants
I saw an anteater reading The Sun
I saw mum.

Danielle King (11)
St Matthew's Junior School, Luton

THE MIRROR

She looks so quiet,
She looks so bright,
With no reflection.

Is she shy?
With so many faces,
Staring down.
She stares back,
So empty and cold.

Sally Cao (10)
St Matthew's Junior School, Luton

BEEF/COW

You kill me for your dinner,
Sometimes you cover me with a thick liquid.
Occasionally I'm on the worldwide news.
I can also be in a sandwich.
I taste scrumptious to you!
What am I?

Answer: beef/cow!

Holly Waterton (11)
St Matthew's Junior School, Luton

MY BIKE

There it was
All shiny and bright
Right in front me
A brand new bike.

I couldn't believe
It was really mine
A bike so great
That looked so fine.

I hopped upon
The comfy seat
The pedals were
Perfect for my feet.

I met my mates
At the park
I must remember
To be back before dark.

We raced along
The tree-lined path
My heart was thumping
I went so fast.

Tears were rolling
Down my face
I couldn't slow down
I had to keep pace.

Me, slow down!
No, never!
I wish I could
Ride my bike forever.

Sheri Bowers (10)
William Austin Junior School

MONSTERS

There are many monsters in this world,
Hairy, scary, big and tall,
Short and fat and even small.

Sea monsters, werewolves, space monsters too,
Big foot Godzilla that live in the zoo.

They're under your bed and inside your shoe,
They're inside your wardrobe and inside your loo.

They eat snot sandwiches with bogey fired bread,
They eat mucus mousse and even your head.

So beware of these monsters,
They'll give you a scare,
Time to wake up,
You had a nightmare.

Naweed Darr (9)
William Austin Junior School

OUR PARENTS

Parents are so kind
Parents are the present to me and you
They cheer you up when you are sad
They help you when you are stuck
They hug when you are asleep
They comfort you when you are ill
They are the most wonderful thing in the world
So help them as they do to you and me.

Sadia Shabir (11)
William Austin Junior School

THE INCREDIBLE HENRY VIII

I am the incredible Henry VIII.
You should see the things I can create
(And I'm only 38).
I can . . .
Sing like a bird
And frighten a herd,
I've played a song called Greensleeves
And killed Anne of Cleves.

I can . . .
Chop my wives heads off
And make myself cough.
They call me the big guy
Because I eat lots of pie
And that's who I am
Right inside.

I can . . .
Do archery like a real man
And I put on the fan,
Wherever I can.

I can . . .
Shoot, kill and fight
With all my might.
I'm the best, that's why they call me
The incredible Henry VIII.
(And I'm only 38).

I'm the best,
You know I'm a pest
The one and only *Henry VIII.*

Jabbar Shah (9)
William Austin Junior School

HEADTEACHERS

My headteacher is so mean,
All the children are so keen.

My headteacher says, 'Don't do this!'
The children just keep on shouting, 'Miss!'

My headteacher has so much to do,
The children, why, they just don't have a clue!

My headteacher has no fear,
When there is a fight near.

When my headteacher is not in the mood,
You'd better watch it and not be rude!

My headteacher doesn't like any mess,
So, make sure you always try your best!

Almas Ghafoor (10)
William Austin Junior School

STARS

Stars are bright
They give us light
With all their might.
They shine at night.

If you make a wish
Upon a wishing star.
It might come true.
Wherever you are.

If you look above
To the sky up high
You are drawn
To the beauty of stars.

Saira Miah (8)
William Austin Junior School

OUR FRIENDSHIP

Who knows us better than our friends,
When we make mistakes,
Friends forgive us when we're down
They lift us up.
And if we move away
They keep a part of us back home.

My heart is like a rose,
A rose split in two,
The leaves I give to others.
The rest I give to you.

A star has five sides and each side represents *you*
One side for your *looks,*
Second for your *charm,*
The third for your *smile,*
The fourth for your *beauty,*
And the fifth for your *friendship.*

Not matter where you are,
No matter how far,
Just call my name
And I'll come in a hurry.
On me you can depend,
And need never worry.

Sanya Akhtar (11)
William Austin Junior School

MY ADVENTURE

On my wonderful adventure,
I saw lots of treasure.
It was the best place,
It was better than going to space.
I had many things to eat,
Like doughnuts, chocolates and sweets.
I saw flowers that were colourful and bright,
The sun shone a light.
In my hand was gold,
When I felt it, it was getting cold.
The river was fresh and clean,
But the people were strange and mean.
I wanted to stay,
Just for one more day.
I had to go home,
The next day I decided to go to the Dome.

Zainab Muneer (10)
William Austin Junior School

A WEAK POEM

Oh dear, this poem is very weak
I can hardly stand up straight
Which comes from eating junk food
And going to bed too late.

Ricky Shah (9)
William Austin Junior School

I FEEL SICK

I feel sick, Mum
What's the matter, son?
I feel ill,
I definitely need a pill.
Are you sure?
Yes, there's puke on the floor.
Mum gave me a pill,
With a glass fill.
I drank it all.
From behind the door I heard Mum's call.
Look at the mess you've made,
It isn't going to fade.
Go get the dustpan and brush,
Hurry, you'd better rush.

Fabian Statchwell (10)
William Austin Junior School

CATS

Cats are clever and can climb trees.
They slurp up milk,
They eat and sleep under tables and in trees.
They like to play with a ball of string.
Cats roll and roll around under your feet.
Cats are soft, cuddly and are the best pet in the world.

Leanne Bricknell (9)
William Austin Junior School

GHOSTBUSTERS!

G hosts are in the city,
H aunting everywhere,
O ften driving people out,
S obbing with despair,
T hen I started a company, the
B est, I often boast,
U sing lasers close in hands,
S o we can kill all ghosts.
T he first ghost we had to deal with
E ats everything it saw,
R eversed the polarity of our lasers,
S o now there's twenty-four!

Zain Yasin (9)
William Austin Junior School

FROM THE PLANET GREEN

From the Planet Green,
There were slugs who do as they please.
Leaving a trail of green,
With little aliens on their backs.

The aliens come to take over the world,
The slugs come to eat all the food,
And both torture the people.

But we on Earth have no need to fear,
Because they're twenty million miles away,
And their top speed is a step a year.

Sheetal Bharadia (10)
William Austin Junior School

SEASONS

Summer
Summer makes me happy
I have fun in every way.
This is when all the children
Go outside to play.
This a time of shines
That brightens up the day.
This is why this is my best season.
I love it, I don't want it to go away.

Spring
Spring I like to see
Because flowers grow pretty for me.
I can sit underneath a tree,
I can see God's creations he has put here for me.

Autumn
Autumn's not such fun for me,
There's always to many leaves.
When the leaves fall off the tree
It's such a sight to see.
Poor old mummy has to clean it up for me.

Winter
Winter is a time of all year round,
Snow, rain and Christmas to carry out good sounds.
It is a time to forgive and forget
And start a brand new year,
That is why all four seasons
Make me want to cheer.

Jaleesa Evelyn (9)
William Austin Junior School

THE RECIPE

This pot contains the official recipe of:
Pot belly custard
And hot mustard.
With lots of spice
And five grains of rice.
Add two pieces of pineapple and make it chuckle.
Mix in lots of honeysuckle.
This makes a custard cake,
Chuck this into a lake.
After an hour take it out,
Put it through a teapot spout.
Make it burn,
Make it turn.

Now you have some dough,
Put it onto a crow.
Now we add lots of sweets,
Put cake or custard not no sleets.
Have you tasted butter?
Put some in and let it flutter.
Sweets are tasty,
Don't be hasty.
Now it's done,
It was fun.
Yum, tum,
Tastes like bubblegum.
Want a taste?
I'll tell you what's best,
Just have a rest.

Sara Shah (10)
William Austin Junior School

AFTER DEATH

One night I was ill,
So I took a pill,
I was allergic to it so I cried,
And then suddenly I died.

I landed in a pit called Hell,
Where they were ringing a very loud bell,
A devil appeared and told me I smell,
It was like being locked in a jail cell.

Then I reached a place called Heaven,
By then the time had reached seven,
The angels offered me a sweet,
They were very nice to meet.

There I picked a sunny spot,
To look down at the cot,
Where I was put beneath the ground,
Without a single crying sound.

They put my ashes in the mud,
With a simple loud thud,
My thoughts and ideas flew in the air,
And I got sent up here with my hair.

Manjit Sobti (10)
William Austin Junior School

FRIENDSHIP

Friends are people who share your love with you.
Friends are a part of your heart.
Friends are people who link up with you.
Friends are who play with you.
Friends are who share secrets with you.
Friends are people who are a part of your life.
Friends cheer you up when you're in stress, upset or emotion.
Friends are who stand up for you when you're in trouble.
Friends are who *care* for you.
Friends make you laugh, cry and smile.
Friends make you think deeply in your heart.
Friends are the people who think deeply about you.
Friends encourage you to do good.
Friends are friends.
Will you be my friend please?

Mariya Shabir (10)
William Austin Junior School

SPIDERS

It's in the bath,
It's on my scarf,
Whatever I say, whatever I do,
It's watching me,
It's watching you.

They come in different sizes,
And are full of surprises.
They're really hairy but really scary,
They're everywhere,
They crawl up the stairs.

I look in pots,
I look in cots,
They're always there,
They don't care,
They're spiders.

Bethany Robins (9)
William Austin Junior School

MY PLANE TRIP

I'm in the aeroplane,
Playing with my game,
High up in the wonderful blue sky,
As clouds fly by,
Looking out of the window,
Wearing my bow,
Cuddling my bear,
Looking at the air.

Loudly chatting way,
Right at midday,
Lunch is coming through,
With chocolate too,
I see a third,
A third bird,
I'm eating lunch,
In front of me there is a flower bunch,
I'm reading a book,
Which my sister took.

Matthew Giddins (9)
William Austin Junior School

FRIENDSHIP

Friends are friends, they are fit,
Then the friendship starts to split.
It starts a real nasty fight,
It makes you stay up in the middle of the night.
If you are stuck, you don't know what to do,
You should make up, if you really want to.
It is better to pick a really true friend,
Not the kind that friendship might end.
Your friend might drive you round the bend,
Now you know what friendship is.
And please, please, please don't let it end.

Samantha Turner (9)
William Austin Junior School

UP, UP AND AWAY

All the planes
Fly in the sky
Very high
Oh very high
The sky is high
Oh very high
So ride on a plane
For you'll go insane!

Keryanne Roxborough (8)
William Austin Junior School